SHEILA DIVERSON

Las Vegas Travel Guide With Kids

Unlock the Ultimate Family Adventure in Las Vegas:
A Kid-Focused Travel Pocket Book

1

Your Family Adventure Awaits

L as Vegas, a city with high stakes and late nights, might not be the first place that comes to mind for a family trip, but here we are, ready to flip the script. I'm your guide on this adventure, a fellow parent who knows the hidden treasures that make Vegas a family-friendly haven. This isn't your typical travel guide; it's a road map for families seeking an unforgettable experience beyond the dazzling lights of the Strip.

Let me introduce myself—I am a parent of three, and I have been a resident of Las Vegas for almost two decades. I've found that there's more to Vegas than what meets the eye. This is a journey into a side of the city that often gets overshadowed by its reputation for excess.

Now, let's cut to the chase. What does this guide offer you? It's not about drowning you in details but providing practical insights to make your Vegas trip memorable. We're talking about kid-friendly shows that will capture your little one's imagination and activities that won't break the bank. I've scouted out the best dining spots to cater to every taste, from sophisticated palates to the fussiest eaters. And I won't confine ourselves to the glittering Strip; we'll explore the hidden gems that await beyond the tourist traps.

So, why should you keep reading? Simple. This is your ticket to making the most out of your family's Vegas adventure. Think of this guide as your practical friend, offering tips and tricks to ensure you don't miss a beat. From navigating the city smartly to uncovering the best spots, I've got you covered.

Let's get down to business. Get set for an adventure where family fun takes center stage. No more waiting—let's dive into the unexpected wonders of the Entertainment Capital of the World.

2

Travel Smart

B efore you hit the dazzling lights of Vegas with your family, it's crucial to set the stage for a smooth ride. In this chapter, we'll break down the essential steps to ensure your trip is not just memorable but stress-free. Let's get practical and dive into the nitty-gritty details that will make your family adventure to Las Vegas a breeze.

Booking Your Flight: Navigating the Skies for Family Value

When it comes to booking flights for your family, a strategic approach can make all the difference. Start by exploring reputable travel websites such as Expedia, Kayak, or Skyscanner, which allow you to compare prices across various airlines. Consider flexibility in your travel dates; flying mid-week or during off-peak hours can often yield more budget-friendly options.

For families of four, costs can vary, but on average, expect to allocate between $300 and $600 per person for a round-trip ticket, depending on your departure location and the time of year. Keep in mind that booking in advance typically offers better deals, so don't procrastinate.

To stretch your budget further, sign up for fare alerts on these platforms or use apps like Hopper to monitor price fluctuations. Timing is key, and these tools can help you snag the best deal when prices drop. Additionally, consider airlines that cater to families, offering perks like early boarding, extra legroom, or complimentary kid-friendly meals.

Opting for a direct flight can be a game-changer, especially when traveling with little ones. While connecting flights might seem like an opportunity to save, the convenience of a non-stop journey can be priceless when you factor in the comfort and ease it provides for both you and your kids.

Finally, don't forget to check the airline's official website. Sometimes, exclusive deals and promotions are available directly through the airline, and loyalty programs may offer additional perks for families. As you embark on this flight-booking mission, remember: a well-planned takeoff sets the tone for a fantastic family adventure.

Traveling By Car

For your family adventure, choosing the open road opens a world of options. Renting a car is easy with platforms like Rentalcars.com and Kayak, offering choices from major players like Enterprise and Hertz. Aim for a midsize SUV or sedan for a family of four, balancing comfort and budget, with daily rates between $40 and $100.

If you're driving your own vehicle, follow three key tips. First, ensure your vehicle is road-ready with proper tire inflation, fluid checks, and brake inspection. Second, plan your route meticulously using navigation apps like Google Maps or Waze to make the journey memorable. Finally, pack strategically—include a cooler for snacks, essential items like a spare tire, jack, and a roadside emergency kit, and entertainment to keep the journey enjoyable.

Arriving from Outside the US

Planning a trip from outside the United States involves careful preparations to ensure a seamless and enjoyable experience for your family. First and foremost, it's crucial to ensure that each family member possesses a valid passport, with attention to expiration dates. Some countries require a specified period of validity beyond your intended stay. Depending on your country of origin, a visa may also be necessary for entry into the United States. It's advisable to initiate the visa application process early, considering potential variations in processing times. The U.S. Department of State's official website provides up-to-date information on visa procedures and entry requirements.

Understanding the time zone difference is another consideration, as Vegas operates on Pacific Standard Time (PST) or Pacific Daylight Time (PDT) depending on the season. Familiarizing yourself with this difference can help minimize jet lag and facilitate a smoother transition into the local rhythm. Prioritizing your family's health is crucial; check for any recommended vaccinations or health precautions for travelers from your region to the United States and stay informed about potential health advisories.

If arriving from a country with a different currency, be mindful of currency exchange and familiarize yourself with current exchange rates. Understanding local customs and etiquette enhances the travel experience. Las Vegas is a diverse city that welcomes visitors from around the world, and being aware of cultural nuances, from tipping practices to social norms, contributes to a more enjoyable stay.

Lastly, keep a record of important emergency contact information, including the details for your country's embassy or consulate in the United States. This information can be invaluable in unexpected situations or if you need assistance during your stay. By addressing these essential aspects before your journey, you set the stage for a stress-free and enjoyable family vacation in Las Vegas, even when arriving from outside the United States. International travel requires careful planning, but with thorough preparations, you'll be ready to embrace the excitement and wonders of the Entertainment Capital of the World.

Budgeting for Your Trip

Setting a realistic budget is a crucial step to ensure that your family's Vegas adventure is not only enjoyable but financially stress-free. Start by estimating expenses, covering flights, accommodation, meals, and activities. Early bookings save money, especially during off-peak seasons. Bundle services for added savings, and explore free or low-cost activities to balance your itinerary.

Set a daily spending limit for meals and miscellaneous expenses, and include a contingency fund for unexpected costs. Utilize credit card rewards and loyalty programs for discounts on flights and hotel stays. Proactive budgeting not only ensures financial ease but also enhances your overall experience in Las Vegas.

Weather: Navigating the Seasons for Your Vegas Adventure

Choosing the perfect time for your family's Vegas adventure is a critical part of the planning process. The optimal time to visit Las Vegas depends on your family's weather preferences and desired activities. Generally, the spring (March to May) and fall (September to November) seasons provide mild temperatures, offering a pleasant outdoor experience with fewer crowds. Summer (June to August) brings scorching heat, making lightweight, breathable clothing, wide-brimmed hats, and sunglasses essential. Winter (December to February) offers cooler temperatures, perfect for indoor activities and holiday festivities.

When packing for your kids, consider layers for spring and fall, ensuring they have light jackets or sweaters for cooler evenings and comfortable sneakers for exploring. In summer, prepare for the heat with lightweight clothing, sun protection gear, and water bottles to stay hydrated. Winter requires layers, including jackets or coats for chilly nights, and don't forget comfortable walking shoes, hats, and gloves for the evenings.

Regardless of the season, sun protection is crucial in Vegas's sunny climate. Pack sunscreen with a high SPF, hats, and sunglasses for the entire family. Staying hydrated is key, so carry reusable water bottles for everyone. Plan a mix of indoor and outdoor activities to balance the temperature extremes, exploring indoor attractions during the hottest or coolest parts of the day. By considering Las Vegas's weather nuances and packing accordingly, you ensure a comfortable and enjoyable family adventure. Whether your crew prefers mild temperatures, the excitement of summer, or the holiday charm of winter, Vegas has something to offer year-round. Dress appropriately and stay sun-smart for a memorable experience.

Where to Stay: Crafting a Family-Friendly Vegas Haven

Selecting the ideal accommodation forms the cornerstone of your family's Vegas adventure. Explore a variety of options, ranging from family-friendly hotels to inviting Airbnb residences, tailored to meet your family's specific needs.

If you're seeking the quintessential Vegas experience with family-friendly touches, consider The Venetian Resort. Known for its spacious suites and charming gondola rides, it sets a lively tone for your stay.

Mandalay Bay Resort and Casino, with its tropical-themed pool area and the Shark Reef Aquarium, is another excellent choice for families. For a touch of medieval magic, Excalibur Hotel & Casino offers a fairy-tale ambiance, complete with a Tournament of Kings dinner show mentioned later in this book and a kid-approved pool complex.

For a more intimate and personalized stay, Airbnb offers an array of choices. Spacious homes with private pools and multiple bedrooms provide a home-away-from-home atmosphere.

Take into account the proximity of your chosen accommodation to family-friendly attractions, ensuring convenience during your stay. Look for amenities specifically designed for kids, such as pools, game rooms, and organized activities. Some hotels even offer babysitting services, allowing parents to enjoy a night out on the town. Consider accommodations with flexible cancellation policies, providing peace of mind in case plans need adjustment. Delve into reviews from fellow family travelers to glean insights into the family-friendliness of a particular hotel or Airbnb listing.

Whether you opt for the glamour of a Strip resort or the coziness of an Airbnb hideaway, your choice of accommodation shapes the comfort and memorability of your family's Vegas experience. Factor in your preferences, explore the diverse options available, and get ready to weave lasting memories in the Entertainment Capital of the World!

Transportation: Navigating Vegas with Ease

Effortlessly navigating Las Vegas enhances your family's adventure, and there are various transportation options to explore. The Regional Transportation Commission (RTC) operates an extensive and efficient bus system covering key areas like the Strip and downtown. Consider the budget-friendly 3-Day All Access Pass for unlimited rides during your stay. Rideshare services like Uber and Lyft offer a convenient and often cost-effective way to get around, ideal for families with the flexibility to choose pick-up and drop-off locations. The Las Vegas Monorail provides a unique and elevated experience, connecting major resorts along the Strip with scenic views. Walking is an excellent option, especially along the iconic Strip, where many attractions are within strolling distance.

For those planning to venture beyond the city limits, renting a car is a practical option, providing flexibility for day trips. Be mindful of traffic, especially on the Strip during peak times, and consider scheduling activities during off-peak hours to avoid congestion. Arrange transportation from the airport to your accommodation in advance for a smooth start to your Vegas adventure. Many hotels offer shuttle services, and taxis, rideshares, and limousines are readily available.

Explore these transportation options, tailor your choices to your family's needs, and effortlessly traverse the city, ensuring every moment of your Vegas adventure is a delight. So, whether you hop on a bus, catch a ride, or glide along the monorail, the Entertainment Capital of the World awaits your family's exploration!

Duration of Stay

Determining your family's ideal stay duration in Las Vegas involves finding a balance between exploration and practical considerations. A 4 to 5-day visit offers a comprehensive experience, allowing leisurely exploration of the iconic Strip, attendance at family-friendly shows, and immersion in various attractions. For shorter weekend getaways, efficient planning is crucial, thanks to Las Vegas's condensed attractions and efficient transportation. Prioritize must-see attractions for an optimized visit. Adjust your stay length based on specific events, maintaining flexibility for spontaneous exploration and considering seasonal variations. Whether planning an extended vacation or a brief escape, ensure every moment is crafted for lasting memories. Pack your sense of adventure and get ready to create unforgettable experiences in

Las Vegas!

3

Kid-Friendly Shows

E mbarking on a family adventure in Las Vegas involves discovering the city's captivating entertainment, and this chapter is your guide to the best kid-friendly shows. Each show promises a unique experience, blending awe-inspiring performances with family-friendly appeal. Before you dive into the enchanting world of Vegas entertainment, here's a breakdown of the must-see shows to enjoy with your little ones.

America's Got Talent Presents Superstars Live!

Dive into the world of live entertainment at "America's Got Talent

Presents Superstars Live!" in the Luxor Hotel. This captivating show brings the best of AGT to the stage, featuring sensational acts from magicians to singers. Kids love the diverse talents, offering a delightful variety of acts for everyone. The visual spectacle and electrifying atmosphere ensure an extraordinary evening. With various ticket options, families can choose based on their budget, from standard views to VIP packages. Arriving early adds to the excitement, making it a memorable and affordable night out. This showcase isn't just a show; it's an immersive experience, promising an unforgettable, family-friendly night in the heart of Vegas.

Blue Man Group: A Unique Fusion of Music, Comedy, and Technology

Dive into a sensory show at the Luxor Hotel with the "Blue Man Group." This family-friendly spectacle uniquely blends music, comedy, and cutting-edge technology, featuring blue-skinned performers in an interactive experience. Kids find this exciting playground with energetic performances and interactive engagement, offering universal appeal. Check for age recommendations, and arrive early to immerse in the pre-show ambiance and explore Luxor Hotel's amenities.

Tournament of Kings: A Medieval Feast of Entertainment

Step into the world of "Tournament of Kings" at Excalibur Hotel. This kid-friendly dinner show is a captivating journey back to medieval times, immersing you in thrilling tournaments and a grand feast fit for royalty. Known for its interactive adventure, kids are particularly drawn to the show's dynamic combination of dinner and entertainment. As valiant knights engage in daring battles, young spectators find themselves part of the action, creating an engaging and immersive experience.

The show is celebrated for its unique blend of interactive elements, ensuring that every member of the family is not just a viewer but an active participant in the medieval spectacle. With its emphasis on audience engagement, "Tournament of Kings" offers more than just a performance; it provides a memorable and interactive adventure that resonates with both children and adults alike. Journey through time as knights showcase their prowess in the arena, bringing the magic of medieval tales to life.

Jabbawockeez: A Dance Extravaganza of Creative Brilliance

Witness rhythmic brilliance at "Jabbawockeez," a dynamic dance show at MGM Grand. This family-friendly performance showcases the iconic Jabbawockeez dance crew, known for their mesmerizing routines and signature masked performances. The show seamlessly blends music, dance, and visual storytelling, creating a captivating experience for all ages.

For children, "Jabbawockeez" offers a visually engaging performance that sparks excitement and creativity. The masked performances add mystery, enhancing the show's appeal for young viewers. The interactive and energetic nature invites children to immerse themselves in rhythm and movement, fostering an appreciation for dance.

Ka By Cirque Du Soleil

Step into the enchanting world of "Ka" by Cirque du Soleil, a mesmerizing spectacle that unfolds at the MGM Grand. Known for its breathtaking blend of acrobatics, storytelling, and innovative stagecraft, "Ka" transports audiences to a realm of imagination and wonder. The show is particularly captivating for kids, offering a visual feast of gravity-defying stunts and awe-inspiring performances that spark their curiosity and fuel their imagination.

"Ka" is renowned for its unique stage, featuring a colossal moving platform that rotates and tilts, creating dynamic landscapes and gravity-defying scenes. The intricate choreography, coupled with the captivating narrative, keeps both adults and children on the edge of their seats throughout the performance. The show's creative use of technology, including stunning projections and special effects, adds a layer of magic to the experience, making it a memorable outing for families.

With a story line that weaves together adventure, love, and heroism, "Ka" engages audiences of all ages, offering a sensory-rich experience that transcends the traditional boundaries of live entertainment.

4

Cost-Free Attractions

Uncover the activities of Las Vegas without spending a dime with our guide to cost-free activities in the city. This chapter is a curated list of places and experiences that won't dent your budget but will enrich your visit. Each subsection provides insight into the location, a detailed description of the activity, and valuable tips to ensure a seamless and enjoyable experience.

The Aquarium at Silverton Casino Hotel

Experience family-friendly fun at the Silverton Aquarium, located conveniently at 3333 Blue Diamond Rd, just a short drive south of the Las Vegas Strip. The marine exhibits features seahorses and tropical fish, offering a glimpse into ocean biodiversity. Interactive feeding shows add excitement, making it an educational outing for kids. The Aquarium, provides vibrant displays and shows, creating a playground of discovery. Don't miss the enchanting live mermaid for a touch of magic, allowing children to capture whimsical memories with these mythical beings. Access is easy—head south from the Las Vegas Strip, turn right onto Blue Diamond Road, and find ample parking at Silverton Casino Hotel. Plan ahead by checking the mermaid show schedule for a stress-free visit.

Bellagio Botanical Gardens

Located within the Bellagio Hotel and Casino at 3600 Las Vegas Blvd S, the Bellagio Botanical Gardens offer families a serene escape in the heart of the city. This botanical oasis seamlessly blends art and nature, presenting a changing tapestry of beauty with each season. Meticulously arranged flowers, plants, and trees create a harmonious display, captivating families as they stroll along the pathways. Throughout the year, the Gardens showcase different arrangements, from spring blooms to autumn foliage, providing a dynamic experience for visitors. One of its remarkable features is that it's a free attraction, offering families a budget-friendly and accessible retreat. Capture seasonal wonders in timeless photographs against the backdrop of nature's artistry. The Gardens stand as an ideal setting for family pictures, where the beauty of nature becomes a vibrant canvas for shared moments. Look out for special events or themed displays for an extra layer of excitement. In the heart of the Las Vegas Strip, the Bellagio Botanical Gardens invite families to the transformative power of nature, providing a tranquil and enchanting experience throughout the seasons.

Bellagio Fountains: A Mesmerizing Waterfront Spectacle

Additionally, in the same location, the Bellagio Fountains redefine the essence of a water feature. This captivating display transforms the bustling Las Vegas Strip into a canvas of aquatic artistry. The fountains, strategically choreographed with a series of water jets, create a dynamic performance enhanced by the backdrop of the Bellagio Hotel and Casino. The central location allows families to seamlessly incorporate the fountain show into their exploration of the Strip, becoming a central part of the city's entertainment scene.

The sophisticated system of water jets is a masterpiece of precision, each movement carefully calibrated to synchronize with a curated selection of music. This elevates the water display beyond a traditional fountain show, turning it into a mesmerizing water symphony. Lights integrated into the water jets add a vibrant array of colors, transforming the fountain show into a visual feast. Whether it's a classic melody, contemporary hit, or a thematic composition, the music enhances the overall experience, creating a multisensory spectacle.

One of the most appealing features of the Bellagio Fountains is it's a free attraction for the entire family. You can gather and enjoy a world-class performance without any cost. While the regular fountain shows are a treat in themselves, it's worthwhile to check the schedule for any special performances or themed displays. They occasionally host unique shows, adding an extra layer of excitement and variety to the regular schedule. Additionally, experiencing the fountains at different times of the day offers distinct perspectives, with the play of sunlight and evening lights adding nuances to the overall spectacle.

The Volcano at The Mirage

Located in front of The Mirage Hotel and Casino at 3400 Las Vegas Blvd S, The Volcano emerges as a captivating free show that transforms the Strip into a theater of fiery splendor. This outdoor spectacle, set against the backdrop of a lagoon, brings the primal beauty of a volcanic eruption to life. The show unfolds with masterful use of pyrotechnics, fire, and water, creating a mesmerizing display that lights up the night sky.

Day or night, The Volcano becomes a focal point, drawing visitors into a multisensory experience. The eruption, simulated with flames shooting into the air creates a dynamic and thrilling atmosphere that captivates audiences of all ages.

Synchronized with the fiery display, The Volcano features a carefully selected musical score that enhances the overall experience. From tribal beats to contemporary compositions, the music complements the visual spectacle, creating a dramatic and immersive atmosphere. Dynamic lighting further amplifies the eruption, transforming the night sky into a canvas of vibrant colors.

The strategic location of The Volcano places it near other notable attractions on the Las Vegas Strip, enriching the overall experience for families. This proximity allows visitors to plan a comprehensive exploration, incorporating nearby hotels, culinary delights, and other free attractions into their itinerary.

Downtown Container Park

T'he Downtown Container Park offers families a unique urban adventure. Located at 707 Fremont St, this innovative attraction is a vibrant hub crafted from repurposed shipping containers, embodying modern design and sustainability. Families exploring the park will encounter a dynamic mix of shops, restaurants, and entertainment spaces housed within these creatively repurposed containers. The modern and eco-friendly design adds a distinctive flair to the surroundings, creating an atmosphere that combines urban chic with a commitment to environmental consciousness.

As families wander through the container maze, they'll discover a diverse range of boutiques, eateries, and galleries, each with its own charm and character. The repurposed containers serve not only as functional spaces but also as artistic canvases, showcasing the creative spirit that defines the heart of downtown Las Vegas. Beyond the unique shopping and dining experiences, the Downtown Container Park caters to families with a dedicated play area for little kids. This thoughtfully designed space provides a safe and engaging environment for children to explore, ensuring that families of all ages can enjoy the urban adventure together. With its blend of modern aesthetics, eco-friendly ethos, and family-friendly offerings, the Downtown Container Park stands as a testament to the dynamic and evolving spirit of downtown Las Vegas.

Flamingo Wildlife Habitat

Escape the hustle of the Las Vegas Strip at the Flamingo Wildlife Habitat, a serene oasis at 3555 Las Vegas Blvd S within the Flamingo Hotel and Casino. This free attraction provides a peaceful and educational retreat for families. The highlight is the flamingo colony, surrounded by koi fish and turtles, offering a tapestry of natural wonders. It serves as both an observation space and an open classroom, allowing parents to share insights about wildlife behaviors and conservation.

As a free attraction, it makes it ideal for families on a budget or those seeking a nature-centric activity. Upon entering, you'll step into a green oasis with well-maintained pathways guiding you through lush vegetation, vibrant flowers, and towering trees—a peaceful retreat.

The Flamingo Wildlife Habitat provides families with a practical and immersive nature experience in Las Vegas. From the elegance of the

C hapter 6 of our guide is a culinary journey through the best dining experiences in Las Vegas catered specifically for families. Discover a selection of top-notch restaurants offering not only delicious dishes but also a kid-friendly atmosphere. From casual bites to savory delights, this chapter provides insights into the best menu items, affordability, and additional information to make dining with your family a memorable experience.

Shake Shack: Casual Delights for the Whole Family

Embrace the laid-back and family-friendly vibes of Shake Shack, a beloved eatery known for its mouthwatering burgers and casual charm.

In three locations (Premium Outlets, Summerlin, and New York New York Hotel), Shake Shack has become a go-to spot for families seeking a relaxed dining experience without compromising on flavor. The restaurant's famous dish, the "ShackBurger," steals the show with its perfectly seared patty, fresh veggies, and signature ShackSauce, creating a burger experience that leaves taste buds dancing.

What sets Shake Shack apart for families is not just the quality of their food but also the kid-friendly options that ensure even the pickiest eaters find something to enjoy. From the classic ShackBurger to the crispy crinkle-cut fries and creamy shakes, Shake Shack crafts a menu that caters to both young and adult tastes. With a welcoming atmosphere and a commitment to using high-quality ingredients, Shake Shack provides families with a memorable and delightful dining experience.

Mon Ami Gabi: French Elegance with a Family-Friendly Twist

Mon Ami Gabi exudes French charm and culinary excellence. Situated in the Paris Hotel, this restaurant seamlessly combines the elegance of French cuisine with a family-friendly atmosphere, making it a top choice for those seeking a touch of sophistication without sacrificing comfort.

A standout on the menu is the classic "Steak Frites," a dish that exemplifies the restaurant's commitment to French culinary traditions. Beyond the delectable menu, what makes Mon Ami Gabi especially appealing for families is its strategic location. Positioned to overlook the iconic Bellagio fountains, dining at Mon Ami Gabi transforms into a free, mesmerizing show for families. Kids not only enjoy the delicious dishes crafted with care but also the enchanting water dance that unfolds just beyond the restaurant's windows.

With its unique blend of French elegance and family-friendly ambiance, Mon Ami Gabi invites families to savor exquisite flavors while creating cherished memories in the heart of Las Vegas.

It's Sushi: A Japanese Feast for the Whole Family

Experience the world of It's Sushi, a Japanese all-you-can-eat restaurant. Two available locations at 4815 Spring Mountain Rd and 8410 West Warm Spring Rd, this lively establishment combines the artistry of sushi with a family-friendly atmosphere, creating an unforgettable dining experience. Their popular signature dish is the "Rainbow Roll," a colorful and flavorful masterpiece that delights both the eyes and taste buds. Families are drawn to the restaurant not only for its delectable sushi options but also for the lively ambiance.

Its Sushi sets the stage for a unique dining experience with fast service and hip, loud pop music that creates an atmosphere akin to a kid-friendly nightclub. The all-you-can-eat concept allows kids to explore a variety of flavors, and the energetic vibe, complete with lively music, transforms the dining experience into a fun-filled dining.

Dive into a world of exquisite flavors at 'It's Sushi' – where artistry meets authenticity in every bite.

Zippy's: A Taste of Hawaii in Las Vegas

Discover the unique flavors of Hawaii at Zippy's, making its mark as the first chain outside of the Hawaiian Islands to bring its culinary delights to Las Vegas. Situated at 7095 Badura Ave, Zippy's offers a tropical escape for families seeking a taste of the Pacific in the middle of the desert.

What makes Zippy's a hit among families is its ability to transport diners to the sun-soaked shores of Hawaii through its diverse menu. Kids, in particular, are drawn to the playful and flavorful offerings that reflect the vibrant Hawaiian cuisine. One of the restaurant's popular dishes, the "Zip Pac," captures the essence of Zippy's culinary expertise. Inside this famous plate, families can enjoy a combination of teriyaki beef, fried chicken, a breaded white flaky fish filet and Spam, accompanied by rice topped with classic Japanese takuan pickled radish and furikake seasoning.

Beyond the delectable menu, Zippy's creates a family-friendly atmosphere that appeals to all ages. The fusion of Hawaiian flavors, friendly service, and the novelty of being the first chain to bring a taste of Hawaii to Las Vegas make Zippy's a must-visit for families seeking a culinary adventure that goes beyond the ordinary.

Catch At The ARIA

Catch, the refined seafood sanctuary tucked away in the heart of ARIA Resort & Casino. With its sleek and contemporary ambiance, Catch delivers not only an exquisite dining experience but also a feast for the senses. The restaurant's modern design sets the stage for a sophisticated meal, making it an ideal destination for families seeking upscale dining.

For the young ones with a penchant for sushi, Catch offers a treat of fresh, high-quality seafood prepared with the same attention to detail as a celebrity's dining experience. The restaurant boasts a visually stunning grand entryway, a floral tapestry that entices visitors and has become a hot spot for Instagram enthusiasts.

As you savor the upscale atmosphere, don't miss the chance to savor their renowned "Catch Roll." This signature dish exemplifies the culinary prowess of the restaurant, fusing diverse flavors and textures into a gastronomic masterpiece. From its stylish setting to its delectable offerings, Catch ensures that every family moment is not only a dining experience but a memorable celebration of taste and aesthetics. So, step into Catch and elevate your family's Las Vegas vacation with a blend of sophistication and culinary excellence.

7

Hidden Gems

C hapter 7 of our guide, "Hidden Gems," is your road map to unforgettable day trips, exploring the lesser-known treasures that make Las Vegas a multifaceted destination. Each subsection crafts a full-day itinerary, ensuring families experience the best of these hidden gems.

Mount Charleston: Alpine Escape

Indulge in an alpine getaway at Mount Charleston, a mere 45-minute to one-hour scenic drive from Las Vegas. Kids will be captivated by the transition from desert landscapes to pine forests along the journey.

Once there, families can partake in seasonal activities—snow play in winter and family-friendly hiking in warmer months. Whether building snowmen or exploring trails like Mary Jane Falls, Mount Charleston offers a refreshing escape with dining options at The Resort on Mount Charleston or picnicking in designated areas. It's a perfect day retreat for the entire family.

Hoover Dam: Practical Adventure

Take a quick trip to Hoover Dam, a 45-minute drive from Las Vegas is all it takes. Dive into the dam's history, learning about its vital role in taming the Colorado River during the Great Depression. Take a guided tour to understand the inner workings. Once you've absorbed the historical insights, extend the day by enjoying lakeside fun at Lake Mead, formed by the dam. Boating, picnicking, and soaking in the serene surroundings make for a perfect post-dam adventure.

Grand Canyon National Park

For a day trip to Grand Canyon National Park, hop in the car for a 2.5-hour drive through awe-inspiring landscapes. Kids will love the vastness and beauty of the canyon, especially from viewpoints like Mather Point and Yavapai Observation Station. Learn about the canyon's history shaped by the Colorado River over millions of years. Keep an eye out for wildlife like mule deer and California condors. Admission costs vary, but the experience of standing on the canyon's rim is worth it. A day at Grand Canyon National Park offers both natural beauty and educational insights for the whole family.

Valley of Fire: Desert Day Essentials

Accessible by a one-hour drive from Las Vegas, the Valley of Fire makes for a practical and captivating day trip. Optimal visits occur during the cooler months, from fall to spring, ensuring a comfortable exploration of the vivid red sandstone formations and ancient petroglyphs.

Upon arrival, families can expect a unique playground for exploration, with trails leading to fascinating glimpses into the region's rich history. Keep an eye out for local wildlife, including bighorn sheep and lizards, adding a touch of natural wonder.

The Valley of Fire caters to all ages, offering photo-worthy vistas, climbing opportunities on distinctive rocks, and scenic trails like Mouse's Tank. Whether you're traversing ancient paths or enjoying a family picnic, this desert destination provides practical and captivating options for a day immersed in nature's wonders.

8

Final Remarks

As we conclude this pocket guide to family adventures in Las Vegas, I hope it serves as a valuable companion for your journey through the vibrant and unexpected facets of the Entertainment Capital of the World. From the dazzling lights of the Strip to the serene landscapes just beyond, Las Vegas has more to offer families than meets the eye.

Whether you are exploring the free wonders like the Bellagio Fountains or venturing into the captivating world of Kid-Friendly Shows, the experiences shared in these pages aim to make your family trip memorable and stress-free. Planning your travel smartly with insights into flights, accommodations, and budgeting ensures that your focus remains on creating cherished moments with your loved ones.

The diverse activities, from the thrilling Adventuredome at Circus Circus to the serene Valley of Fire, showcase the versatility of Las Vegas as a family destination. We've delved into the city's rich history, from the engineering marvels of Hoover Dam to the natural wonders of Grand Canyon National Park. Each chapter is crafted to empower you with practical insights, making your family adventure seamless and enjoyable.

As you set out on your Las Vegas journey, don't forget to check out the culinary delights at the Best Dining Restaurants, adding a flavor-filled dimension to your trip. The Hidden Gems chapter unveils day trips that promise to unveil the lesser-known, yet equally spectacular, facets of this dynamic city.

Your feedback is appreciated, and I encourage you to share your thoughts on Amazon. Your reviews not only guide fellow travelers but also contribute to the continual improvement of this guide. Your family adventure in Las Vegas awaits, and I'm honored to be a part of your travels. Here's to making memories that last a lifetime!

9

Resources

Jurga. (2023, September 8). *Family Road Trip Packing List (+Essentials for Kids & What Not To Pack)*. Full Suitcase Travel Blog. https://fullsuitcase.com/packing-road-trip/

Legner, L. (2022, April 22). *Kids' screen time: How much is too much? | OSF HealthCare*. OSF HealthCare Blog. https://www.osfhealthcare.org/blog/kids-screen-time-how-much-is-too-much/#:~:text=Yousuf%20said%20pediatricians%20generally%20recommend,per%20day%2C%20except%20for%20homework

Las Vegas Climate, Weather By Month, Average Temperature (Nevada, United States) - Weather Spark. (n.d.). Weather Spark. https://weatherspark.com/y/2228/Average-Weather-in-Las-Vegas-Nevada-United-States-Year-Round

Las Vegas Monorail. (2023, October 10). *Official route map of the Las Vegas monorail*. https://www.lvmonorail.com/route-map/

Enjoy the Discovery Children's Museum in Las Vegas. (2023, November 4).

Travel Nevada. https://travelnevada.com/childrens-museums/discove
ry-childrens-museum/

The High Roller - Las Vegas Observation Wheel | The LINQ Hotel. (n.d.).
Caesars Home Page. https://www.caesars.com/linq/things-to-do/attr
actions/high-roller

Directions and parking information for visiting Seven Magic Mountains.
(2023, March 9). Seven Magic Mountains. https://sevenmagicmountai
ns.com/visit/

Maxtour. (2023, January 14). All Your Questions Answered about
Visiting Seven Magic Mountains. *MaxTour.* https://www.maxtour.co/
all-your-questions-answered-about-visiting-seven-magic-mountains/
#:~:text=How%20Much%20Did%20Seven%20Magic,Aria%20Hotel%2
0in%20Las%20Vegas.

Shelby Heritage Center. (n.d.). https://www.shelby.com/en-us/Shelby-L
as-Vegas/Shelby-Heritage-Center-Home

Grand Canyon National Park (U.S. National Park Service). (n.d.). https://w
ww.nps.gov/grca/index.htm

Grand Canyon National Park (U.S. National Park Service). (n.d.). https://w
ww.nps.gov/grca/index.htm

Golf, party venue, sports bar & restaurant | TopGolf Las Vegas. (n.d.).
Topgolf. https://topgolf.com/us/las-vegas/?gad_source=1&gclid=Cj0
KCQiAjMKqBhCgARIsAPDgWlyQQucy0EvvuM74cX_iZnKcG7wJ8
D4FqLg2ozXm-B5lq20mjB3yTBkaAqQTEALw_wcB&gclsrc=aw.ds

McFarland, K. (2023, October 11). *Customers pack Hawaiian favorite Zippy's in Las Vegas for grand opening.* Channel 13 Las Vegas News KTNV. https://www.ktnv.com/news/customers-pack-hawaiian-favorite-zippys-for-grand-opening

Thayer, K. (2022, September 9). Catch ARIA: Dining Destination for Celebrities (And You) - OnTheStrip.com. *OnTheStrip.com.* https://www.onthestrip.com/dining/catch-aria-vegas/

Printed in Great Britain
by Amazon